Learn to Pray

A Guide For Young People

Julie Kelemen

Liguori
ONE LIGUORI DRIVE
LIGUORI MO 63057-9999

In Memory of
Rev. Leila Fischer

*Thank you, God,
for all she taught me
about you
and about prayer*

∞

Imprimi Potest:
James Shea, C.Ss.R.
Provincial, St. Louis Province
The Redemptorists

Imprimatur:
Monsignor Maurice F. Byrne
Vice Chancellor, Archdiocese of St. Louis

ISBN 0-7648-0670-X
Library of Congress Catalog Card Number: 00-101065

© 1992, 2000, Julie Kelemen
Printed in the United States of America
00 01 02 03 04   5 4 3 2 1

All rights reserved. No part of this booklet may be reproduced, stored in a retrieval system, or transmitted without the written permission of Liguori Publications.

This booklet was previously published under the title *Prayer Is for Children: Stories, Activities, Prayers,* © 1992 by Liguori Publications.

To order, call 1-800-325-9521
http://www.liguori.org

Cover design by Grady Gunter
Interior art by Chris Sharp

Table of Contents

A Note to Adults 4
A Note About Footnotes 6
1. What Do You Think of Prayer? 7
   Attitudes and Tall Tales About Prayer
2. Prayer Doesn't Happen
   Only When You're Kneeling 17
   What Is Prayer?
3. "Ladies and Gentlemen, Introducing..." 29
   Famous People Who Prayed
4. Why Do So Many People Want to Do This? 39
   Why People Pray
5. What's Your Favorite Flavor? 49
   Different Ways to Pray
6. Is It Really Worth It? 65
   Common Problems With Prayer
Amen 80

A NOTE to Adults

When my first two books (*Lent Is for Children* and *Advent Is for Children*) hit the market, something happened that I had not expected: adults were reading them, too. It was the ultimate compliment to me to have a mother of grown children whose husband was not Catholic say, "I, myself, learned a lot from your book. So did my husband. It explained things so clearly and simply about what the Church teaches. And it was fun reading it!"

No matter how old we get, there is still a child living deep within each of us. That child needs nurturing and attention. That child needs to have fun. That child needs spiritual information and inspiration in small doses rather than via three-pound theological treatises. And that child is the person we must allow to come forward as we communicate with God in prayer. Growing up is no excuse for having no need for God. But you probably already know that, don't you.

Unfortunately, kids and adults alike often think that spiritual matters must always be SERIOUS: "We must pray with a stern, pained look on our faces OR ELSE!" But there is much joy to be found in Christianity, and God wants us to experience that joy when we pray.

If you bought this booklet for your child, I suggest you read it, too. Follow along with your child, even to the point of getting involved in the activities. If you're a teacher who bought this book for students, the same goes for you. Thank God that personal education does not have to stop once we have a teaching certificate, M.B.A., Ph.D., or some other sheepskin in hand.

P.S. Don't feel guilty if you enjoy reading this book!

A Note About Footnotes

This booklet will have footnotes. Since you may have never seen a footnote before, here's one right now:[1] Now look at the bottom of this page for the number 1, and you can read the footnote.

A footnote is like a little clue. It tells you there's something extra to know and that if you'd like to know it, all you need do is match the number up here with the number down there and then you can get a SECRET MESSAGE! (Well, it's not *really* secret, since everyone can read it.)

In this booklet, footnotes will show you when something you're reading comes from the Bible. For example: "...and the frogs came up and covered the land of Egypt."[2] At the bottom of this page, footnote 2 says, "Exodus 8:2." That means if you want to find where this Bible saying comes from, you need to look in the Book of Exodus, chapter 8, verse 2.

Now you know how to use footnotes! (And you didn't even have to take off your shoes!)

---

[1] Hi there! I'm a footnote!
[2] Exodus 8:2

❶ What Do You Think of Prayer?

Attitudes and Tall Tales About Prayer

Look at the pictures of the various children on this page. Put a checkmark beside the picture of the child who best matches your attitude toward prayer. Don't be afraid to tell the truth, because nobody's looking at this but you. If you're not happy with your answer, that's okay. God will help you do better if you just ask.

Your Attitude About Prayer Is Important

Different people think different things about prayer. Your grandma may think it's the greatest thing since pitted prunes (and it is). However, other folks may think it's dumb, boring, not "cool," or useless. They're the kind of persons who probably don't pray much, if at all, or they may be persons who have had a very difficult life. As a result, they may think God has forgotten them, so they talk with God very little if at all.

Your feelings about prayer are important. God wants to be very close to you. God wants to know about what you are thinking, feeling, learning, and all the other things that any good friend might want to know about you. Whenever you let God know about any of these things, that is prayer. If you ever find yourself wondering about things like who God is, where God lives, what God is like, or why God made elephants gray, chocolates delicious, and mice with long skinny tails, *that* can be prayer, too. Anytime you wonder about why God does things a certain way, you are, in a way, asking God questions. If you listen hard, you may even find answers.

Tall Tales About Prayer

A tall tale is a story that's so incredible, it can't be true. A tall tale usually tries to get you to believe something that isn't exactly right. It's like a story your grandfather might tell about a man whose moustache was so long that its tips dragged in the mud all the time. There are some tall tales about prayer out there, too. Here are some of the most common tall tales about prayer.

God is like Santa Claus. People who see God as Santa Claus (or Father Christmas as he's called in some places) tend to pray only when they want something.

"Dear God, I really need a bike...."

"Dear God, make the kids at my new school like me...."

"Dear God, I can't do my math homework; please help me learn...."

Of course, there's nothing wrong with saying prayers like these. God wants to help you and wants to know what your needs are. But if this is the only way you pray, then you see God as a Santa to whom you can take your wish list. But there's a problem with this: what happens if you don't get what you ask for? Does that mean God isn't listening? Does that mean God doesn't like you? Does that mean there is no God? No! But it does mean that you have more to learn about God.

People who see God only as a Santa Claus can get very sad or angry when God doesn't seem to give them exactly what they want. There are a lot of folks like that in the world. These persons usually don't go to church anymore. They may believe God deserted them because they didn't get exactly what they wanted when they needed it. These angry and sad persons aren't bad; after all, what they wanted from God may have been something very important. Perhaps they wanted God to heal their dying mother, keep their parents from getting a divorce, or help them get a job they really needed.

These types of persons really need to get to know Jesus and how much he loves them, because deep down they fear

God doesn't love them or even hates them. If you know someone like this, try to do what Jesus tells us to do: "Love one another. As I have loved you, so you also should love one another. This is how all will know that you are my disciples, if you have love for one another."[3] Jesus wants us to "be Jesus" for others who really need him.

So, if you run across a crabby person in your everyday adventures, remember that the person is crabby because things probably are not going his or her way. Try to give that person a smile, even if it's the furthest thing from your mind at the time. Sometimes all it takes for a crabby or sad person to remember that God is good and loving is to come into contact with someone like you. Sometimes someone who has turned away from God only needs an invitation to come back. And you could offer that invitation.

God is like a Sherman tank. During World War II in the 1930s and 1940s, a tank that American soldiers used was called the *Sherman tank*. It weighed thirty-four tons and had room for four men inside to operate it. Obviously, if you got in the way of a Sherman tank, you were history.

---

[3] John 13:34-35

Now what in the world could a tank have to do with God and prayer? Well, there were probably persons fighting in that war who prayed that a Sherman tank wouldn't destroy them, but that's not what we're talking about here. What we're talking about is how some persons approach prayer as if God were a Sherman tank; they try to "climb inside" God. They use God and prayer like tools to help them get whatever they want.

There's a problem with this attitude, too. Sometimes what *we* want for ourselves and what *God* wants for us are two very different things. For example, *you* may want very badly for someone in your class to like you, and you pray for that to happen. However, *God* may want you to be friends with someone else who could use your friendship much more. Now, if you had the Sherman-tank attitude toward prayer, you might be ticked off at God for not helping you get the friend you want. A person without the Sherman-tank attitude might pray, "Okay, God…so you don't seem to want me to have Anne Marie as a friend. I wish you did, but you don't. What *do* you have in mind for me? Do you want me to stop worrying so much about making friends? Am I supposed to make friends with someone else? What do you want for me, God? Help me know and understand so I can do your will."

Basically, it is important for us to keep in mind that we are here on earth to do God's work and to be "agents" of God living in the world. God does not exist just to help us get our own way all the time. God loves you and me and everyone else in the world in a way that is so perfect and powerful that no human could love us as well. Because God loves us so much and because God knows so much more than we do, God knows what's best for us — even more than we do.

Think about when you first learned to walk. (You may not

remember that time, but just think about what it might have been like.) When you first learned to walk, you probably loved to toddle all over the place. But Mom or Dad also had to keep you from trying to walk down the stairs too soon or else you would have hurt yourself. If Mom or Dad stopped you from walking down the stairs, you might have been angry and cried. (Babies are famous for doing that.) But Mom or Dad knew what was best for you, even though they didn't let you do what you wanted to do — just like God.

God is like an ambulance. Gena just couldn't figure out how to do long division in her math class. No matter how hard she listened to the teacher and tried to follow the directions in the textbook, long division made no sense. She asked her dad, but he would just get frustrated and end up doing a lot of hollering and not much teaching. Gena didn't want to ask her classmates to help her; she worried that they would think she was dumb if she asked them for help. She was afraid they'd make fun of her. It seemed like no one was so stuck as Gena.

In class one day during a math test, Gena got so desperate that she stretched her neck out a bit and caught sight of some answers on Neil's paper. She copied them on her own paper. "Finally!" she thought. *Finally, I'll get some answers right. Neil knows everything.*

But just as she settled back in her seat, the teacher, Mrs. Barco, called out, "Gena, would you please come up to my desk."

Caught!

Mrs. Barco sent Gena to the principal's office. The principal sternly explained to Gena how she could be held back a grade for failing to do her own work. This wasn't the first time Gena had done something against the rules.

When the principal stepped out for a moment to call Gena's parents, Gena put her head in her hands and wept bitterly. Finally, she began to pray: "Please God! Don't let them hold me back a grade. I'll do anything — anything — if only you'll just let me pass to sixth grade. Oh, please, God. I'm in so much trouble. Please help me! Please! Please! Please...."

Gena was in pretty big trouble, wasn't she. She really needed God because she felt she had nowhere else to turn. Her style of praying in this story is a good example of seeing God as an ambulance. Think about it...when do we usually call an ambulance? We usually call an ambulance only when the condition of someone's body is so bad that we can't do anything to help and we need experts: doctors and nurses. We call an ambulance when all else has failed.

Many people see God and prayer as something of an ambulance. They rely on themselves and others to solve all of life's problems and rarely think about God until a real emergency comes along that they can't handle. *Then* they call on God.

Certainly, there's nothing wrong with calling on God when you're in a real pinch. But God likes to hear from you during less stressful times, too. Indeed, if you keep God in your ordinary life every day with some form of prayer, you'll be less likely to end up with major problems like Gena's.

Prayer doesn't need to be a "last resort"; it can be — and should be — a "first resort"!

Is Prayer Only for Weak Persons?

Lee walked into her family's living room one evening to find her father and brothers planted in front of the TV watching a baseball game. Although she didn't understand much about the game, she was willing to learn.

As she munched on some popcorn from the bowl beside her father's armchair, she noticed something she'd never seen before in a ball game. As a batter situated himself by home plate, he stopped for a moment to bless himself with the Sign of the Cross.

"Why did he do that?" Lee asked everyone in the room.

"He's praying that he hits a home run," her brother Vince said.

"Yeah," chuckled Jay, Lee's other brother. "But what if the pitcher is praying to throw a strikeout?"

"I think the batter is probably praying that he just does his very best and that he plays a good, fair game," said Lee's dad.

Now none of us can really know what's in any ballplayer's mind and heart when he blesses himself like that. But the important point is that he blessed himself. He wasn't embarrassed to do it in front of the umpire, the other players, and TV cameras broadcasting his image all across the continent.

Many professional athletes say that they take time to pray while the national anthem is being played. Football teams often pray in their locker rooms before games.

Do all these persons pray to win? Not usually; they usually ask God to be with them, to help them play fair and to their best ability.

With all those big, tough guys out there who care enough to make God a part of their lives through prayer, can you believe there are *still* some persons who think prayer is only for wimps? There are. Boy! Some people!

The truth is, persons who pray are actually often quite strong. Some are physically strong with big muscles and the ability to outrun or outjump just about everyone. Some persons are very strong in other ways; for example, a mother with four young children can manage to be a good mom even if the children's father dies somehow. The fact is, prayer makes you strong in mind and spirit. Those who *don't* think they need God can end up feeling weak from all the problems life has to offer.

Something to Do
Finding the Right Attitude Toward Prayer

The Bible has many things to say about how and why we should talk with God in prayer. Some of those things can be found in the Bible passages below. Look up each Bible passage and see what it says. If you don't know how to find Bible passages, ask someone to teach you. It's fun and easy. You can make a game out of it, if you like, by seeing if you can find, read, and write each passage in fifteen minutes or less.

- Matthew 6:6
- Mark 11:24
- 1 Samuel 3:1-18
- Luke 18:1-7
- Sirach 37:15
- Ephesians 6:18

Prayer for Kids Who Want God to Be Their Friend

Hi, God. It's me. Help me remember that you are always with me, that you want to be part of my everyday life. Even when I'm doing everyday things like brushing my teeth or playing with the dog, I know that you are with me just like any good friend would be. I want to remember to make you a part of my everyday life, not just when there's an emergency or when I want something or when I'm trying to get my own way. With your help, I know I will learn the right attitudes toward prayer.

AMEN

❷
Prayer Doesn't Happen Only When You're Kneeling

What Is Prayer?

Do you know what a Model T Ford is? It's a very old car. Have you ever seen one for real? Someone who has a Model T Ford usually takes very good care of it and may display it in parades and special shows.

Anything that is old but still valuable and wonderful is called a *classic*. A car can be a classic. Some old movies are classics, like *The Wizard of Oz*. An old story like *Robin Hood* is a classic. Old things become classics when people continue to enjoy them or find them helpful, no matter how old those things get.

Here are some classic pictures of famous holy people at prayer.

Mary praying **Jesus praying** **An ancient monk praying**

What do the persons in the pictures on the previous page have in common? They are all on their knees. You've probably knelt in church to pray, too. Knees and prayer go together like bacon and eggs. You can have one without the other, of course. A boy on his knees isn't necessarily praying (maybe he lost something), and a girl who's praying isn't necessarily on her knees (maybe she's riding the school bus).

Many people kneel to pray because that's how they were taught to pray. Praying on your knees is a classic. But where did this praying-on-knees stuff come from? Well, when we kneel, we are honoring Someone or Something Else greater than ourselves. Back in the days when kings and queens were more common than they are now, people often knelt before them. This was to show respect and obedience to the ruler. Likewise, when we kneel to pray, we are showing that we respect God as a Being who is very loving and powerful. This doesn't mean that we're real crumbs or anything bad like that. Kneeling during prayer just reminds us that we don't always have all the answers and that we want to approach God to admit that.

But prayer can happen just as naturally when you're off your knees as when you're on them. God's ears don't slam shut if you're not on your knees to pray. Praying can happen anywhere, anytime, and in any position — even if you're standing on your head!

Something to Do
Hunting for Secret Pray-ers

Dig up some old newspapers or news magazines. Make sure they are ones that you're allowed to cut pictures out of. Page through them and find five or more pictures of persons who *could* be praying. Even if the words near a picture *say* the person is doing something else, don't pay attention to that. Instead, pay attention to the *pictures:* the people, the expressions on their faces, and what their bodies are doing.

Usually, anyone who is being still in some way could be praying. Perhaps a cowboy rustling up cattle or a person making a speech *could* be praying, but it's doubtful. That's because they're obviously *doing* something. Prayer takes concentration. It's hard to focus your mind on praying if the rest of you is lassoing a heifer or talking about the nation's economy.

After you've cut out the pictures of people who could be praying, paste them on a piece of paper and hang it in your classroom, in your bedroom, or on the refrigerator — anyplace where you'll see it often. This will help remind you that prayer can happen anywhere and at anytime.

The Difference Between Prayers and Prayer

The words *prayers* and *prayer* look like they should mean the same thing, don't they. But there can be a difference.

Prayers are those often-memorized verses that you say at mealtime, at bedtime, in church, and maybe at other times, too. You can read prayers in books, or you can make them up on your own. You can say them out loud, or you can say them silently.

Prayer, on the other hand, is bigger than just saying words, whether aloud or in your heart. Prayer can also be a way of *looking* at things, people, events, and the world around you. Whenever something or someone makes you think of God or Jesus or Mary or any of the saints, that is a time of prayer.

Pablo Visits the Park

Pablo lives in an apartment building in Chicago, a big city. When he wants to play ball, he either has to do it at the playground or out in the alley behind the apartment building. His experience in the big park by Lake Michigan is an example of prayer.

* * * * *

"Mama, Papa, why can't we have a house with a backyard?" Pablo has often asked.

"We are saving our money for one," his parents always explain.

Sometimes Pablo and his sister get a big treat. When the weather is nice, Mama and Papa take the family to the big park over by Lake Michigan.

One sunny fall day, Pablo and his papa were running in the park playing Frisbee. At one point, Pablo threw the yellow disk badly, and it landed deep in some thick bushes. As Papa clawed through the bushes, Pablo looked up at the trees glowing with warm fall colors of yellow, orange, and red. Out on the lake bobbed some pretty boats, their brightly colored sails puffing out in the breeze.

The lake's waves broke into white splashes as they neared the beach. A man jogged by with Pablo's favorite kind of dog trotting along behind: an Old English sheepdog. Pablo took a deep breath and caught a whiff of hot tamales that a nearby vendor was selling.

As Pablo's father fished around in the bushes looking for the Frisbee, Pablo simply stood still, soaking in all the wonderful things around him. He knew that this was life, and he knew that this was good. He wanted this Saturday afternoon in the park to last a long, l-o-n-g time. He didn't want Papa to find the Frisbee. He didn't want the jogger and dog to run away. He wanted to command the waters to stay just the way they were and the sun never to set. He wanted to freeze the moment, put it in his pocket and keep it forever. He had never looked at things this way before. It excited him. Then he suddenly remembered something... *God.*

Is this what God can do? Pablo thought to himself.

Papa found the Frisbee and hurled it back to his son. Pablo ran and jumped high into the air and caught the flying disk with one hand!

"Hooray!" Pablo and his father yelled. Pablo jumped up and down and threw the plastic disk high into the air. "I did it! I did it!" Pablo continued jumping and running all over the open grassy field, thinking, *Hooray for today, God! Hooray! You gave me the park and Papa and the tamales and the pretty trees and the sailboats and my favorite dog. Hooray for you, God! Thank you and hooray!*

"Pablo! What are you doing?" his sister, Andrea, called out. She and Mama were bringing hot tamales from the vendor.

"I'm happy! Hooray! I caught the Frisbee," Pablo said, and began running circles around his mother and sister.

"You're *weird!*" said Andrea.

"Slow down!" said Papa.

But Pablo knew he wasn't weird. He just loved the good earth and God who made it. He finally sat down with his family to eat the tamales. Pablo knew he'd remember this day for a long time.

* * * * *

Have you ever had a day like Pablo's? Do you think Pablo was weird? Was Pablo praying? You bet Pablo was praying, even though no one but God and Pablo knew it! Prayer is not just words; prayer is an *attitude,* too. Whenever you think about God, appreciate God, wish you knew more about God, or anything like that, that is a prayerful attitude. Prayer is not just saying words; it is much bigger and better than that.

Have you ever known someone with a "bad attitude"? What about someone with a "good attitude"? What *is* an attitude?

An attitude is your outlook on life. For example, if you think it's good to be friendly and helpful and you work hard to get things done, people will say you have a "good attitude." But if you think being selfish, bullying others, and doing little work are what's right, then others will say you have a "bad attitude." An attitude is your way of looking at the world.

Prayer is an attitude, too. It's a way of looking at the world. Pablo had a good, prayerful attitude in the park, even though he wasn't on his knees and even though he wasn't reciting the Our Father or Hail Mary.

Aren't Persons Who Pray Weird?

Another thing the story about Pablo shows us is that some persons might think you're weird if you have a prayerful attitude. Andrea said Pablo was weird because he was jumping for joy so much...and she didn't even know he was praying. (But then she was his *sister*. It's pretty normal for sisters and brothers to tell each other they're weird, even if it's not nice.)

Are you afraid that others will think you're weird if you pray? If so, you're in good company. *Lots* of people are afraid of that, including the person who wrote this book. That's why so many people pray in private, when no one else is around to bother them.

If you're afraid people will think you're weird if you pray, remember this: *everyone is different*. That means people have different tastes. Your favorite flavor of ice cream may be chocolate, while your mom's favorite is pistachio. Maybe your best friend's favorite musical group is the Screaming Blue Philodendrons, while yours is KTZ-993. If someone says you're weird for liking chocolate ice cream or KTZ-993, is that any reason to stop eating your favorite ice cream or listening to your favorite group? Of course not. It just means you have different tastes.

The same thing is true for prayer. If anyone makes fun of you for praying or wanting to pray, try not to worry about it. Just think of it as the two of you having different tastes. If a friend gives you a hard time about praying or any of your beliefs, then it's time to find a new friend who has tastes more like yours.

Praying is nothing to be ashamed of. In fact, a lot of folks will admire you if they know you pray. They may not say it to you, but that doesn't matter. We don't pray to get others to tell us how good we are. We pray to praise God and to talk with God. That's the only good reason for praying. When we pray, we're following Jesus' good example, because Jesus was a man who prayed an awful lot.

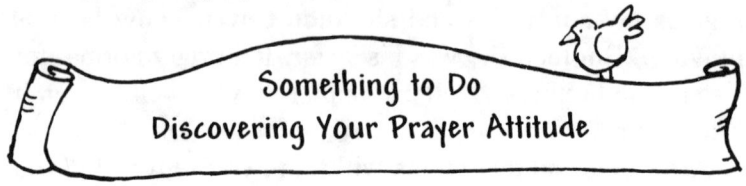

Something to Do
Discovering Your Prayer Attitude

Below are thirteen statements. After each statement, there are two lines; the first is marked "agree" and the second is marked "disagree." If you **agree** with the statement, put an "X" on the first line after the statement. If you **disagree** with the statement, put an "X" on the second line. This quiz will help you see how much of a prayerful attitude you have. Base your answers on what you *really* think. Don't just say what your teacher or parents or even God might want you to say. By being honest, the quiz can help you to be a better "pray-er."

1. Quiet is okay. The TV or radio doesn't always have to be playing.
    Agree_____ Disagree_____
2. Human beings are more valuable than all the money in the world.
    Agree_____ Disagree_____
3. Thinking is okay. I don't always have to be *doing* something.
    Agree_____ Disagree_____
4. There is more good in the world than bad.
    Agree_____ Disagree_____

5. It's good to listen, not just talk.
   Agree_____   Disagree_____
6. No matter how many problems I have, God loves me and helps me.
   Agree_____   Disagree_____
7. Sitting (or standing or laying) and just looking at the world around me is good.
   Agree_____   Disagree_____
8. It's good to pay very close attention to whatever I'm doing.
   Agree_____   Disagree_____
9. Making mistakes is human and Jesus understands.
   Agree_____   Disagree_____
10. Feeling sad, happy, lonely, angry, or other emotions is human and okay.
    Agree_____   Disagree_____
11. I don't have all the answers to my problems. Sometimes I need help.
    Agree_____   Disagree_____
12. While it's good to prepare for the future, I can't spend all my time preparing. I must learn to depend on God and others for help at times.
    Agree_____   Disagree_____
13. I can't completely control how everything in my life turns out. Sometimes I must just let go and let God take care of things.
    Agree_____   Disagree_____

Scoring: Count how many *agree* answers you have. Then match that number with one of the groupings below.

10 or more *agree* answers: You are well on the way to having a healthy, prayerful attitude toward life.

6 to 9 *agree* answers: You're about average. In some ways you're doing well. To have a more prayerful attitude, work on believing some of those statements you disagree with. Take them to God in prayer and ask God to help you believe them.

5 or fewer *agree* answers: You might have what people call a "bad attitude." That doesn't mean you're a bad person, though. It just means that if you want to have a happier life, work on believing more of the statements above. It could also mean that you're very sad or angry about something that has happened to you or something that you've done. If that's true, talk privately about it with a grownup you trust. Talking to a priest you like might be good, too.

Prayer Is Listening, Too

Prayer is basically communication with God.

Communication is a big word that you've probably heard before. Many people think communication means getting a message across to others. They may call a man a "great communicator" if he can easily get others to think and do what he wants by what he says.

But getting a message across is only half of what communication really is. The other half of good communication is *listening.* To be a good communicator, you must be both a good talker *and* a good listener.

In a similar way, many people think of praying as talking *to* God, Jesus, Mary, or the saints, and that is partly true. But praying also involves *listening*. You'll find out more about listening as prayer when you read the Bible story about the boy named Samuel (in the next chapter).

Listening for God doesn't mean that you'll hear a big booming voice or thunder in the clouds or any of that Hollywood-kind of stuff. Listening to God means looking for God and God's goodness in everyday life. For example, when Pablo found himself thinking about God, he was in a way listening to God. Whenever you want to do things for others, you're listening to Jesus' message that we must love one another as he loves us.

Something to Do
Finding a Word for Prayerful Listening

During a time of quiet prayer, sharpen your prayer listening skills by closing your eyes and thinking about how much you love God and how much God loves you. If you find that hard, don't worry. Even grownups find this hard sometimes. When most persons try to do this, they end up thinking about things that have nothing to do with praying: what they need to buy at the store, what they watched on TV last night, or a great joke someone told them. If this sort of thing happens to you (and it probably will), think of a secret word you can use between you and God. It should be a short word like *peace* or *love* or *light*. (Long words like *extemporaneous* or *pulchritudinous* just won't cut it. Don't try those words.) While you're praying, your mind may wander to thinking about a football game or what's for dinner. If this happens, just say your secret word to yourself. It will help bring you back into God's presence. This is something that takes practice, but you *can* do it. Remember, you always get better at things when you practice. This type of praying is especially useful when you're angry, worried, tense, or afraid. It can help you cool down and feel better.

Prayer for Kids Who Are Afraid Prayer Is Weird

Jesus, were you ever afraid to pray? Sometimes I'm afraid to pray because I don't want my friends or family to think I'm some holy-holy weird person. I want to do the right thing and follow you whenever I can, but sometimes it's hard. I'm afraid that if other kids know that I pray or want to pray, they will think I'm weird. Help me remember that *you* don't think I'm weird, and that's the most important thing. Help me remember that I can pray anytime and anyplace. Nobody has to know about it if I don't want them to. I want to remember that it's never weird to be close to you.

AMEN

❸
"Ladies and Gentlemen, Introducing..."
Famous People Who Prayed

Have you ever watched a famous person walk through a crowd? The famous person may have been someone running for president, a woman whose musical recordings have sold millions, an athlete, a queen, a rock star, or a popular person from television or the movies. When famous people walk through a crowd, police officers often have to hold fans back so they don't get too close to the famous person. Fans will hold out their hands and try to touch the famous person.

Flashbulbs on cameras flare everywhere. People make signs that say things like *We Love You, Bonzo!* Some people even get so excited that they scream!

Have *you* ever wished you were famous? What would you like to be famous for? It's pretty normal for regular persons to wish they were famous. That's because if you're famous, lots of people really like you and you often have lots of money.

But there's a downside to being famous, you know. It can be very hard to have a private life when you're famous. Simple things like going out for a walk, eating in a restaurant, or going shopping can be big hassles for famous persons. That's because wherever they go, people stare at them, ask for autographs, and try to take pictures. That's why lots of land and big fences or walls often surround famous persons' houses...so they can have a private life, too.

Jesus: The Famous Man Who Took Time to Pray

Jesus was one of the most famous persons who ever walked on this earth. It's been about two thousand years since that time, and people *still* talk about him! People gather in crowds to praise him and keep his sayings close to their hearts. Even when Jesus was here on earth, he became famous, as he gave eyesight to persons who were blind, cured the persons who had diseases, brought life back to persons who had died, and performed many other miracles. As Jesus did this, sure enough, the crowds following him grew larger. After a while, the apostles tried to keep people away from Jesus because they would crowd him so much. As Jesus' fame grew, it became harder for him to find private time to rest or pray.

When the apostles told Jesus that his cousin, John, had been brutally killed, "he withdrew in a boat to a deserted place by himself."[4] But even when he did that, the crowds followed him.

Just like any other human being, Jesus occasionally needed time away to rest and refresh himself. Whenever he did this, he also took time to be with God in prayer. Many times when lots of folks were making a big fuss over him, he simply went away to pray. Jesus needed time alone to pray and be with God — and so do we.

Like all of us, Jesus had good days and real "crudball" days. He had to deal with folks who *didn't* like him, as well as with folks who thought he was great. There were days when Jesus had too much to do and days when things were more settled. Everyone's life is like that. Jesus is the best example we have for a famous, busy person who took time to pray.

In addition to taking time to pray, Jesus also had a prayerful *attitude*. When someone did something that could have hurt his feelings, Jesus didn't try to get even or yell at the person or anything like that. Instead, he was calm and had something loving or thought-provoking to say to the person. Then he moved on and pretty much forgot about the whole thing.

Also, Jesus didn't spend a lot of time planning for what he would do the next day or the next week. Instead, he lived one day at a time. Jesus wandered from town to town with the apostles. As he did, he stayed watchful for opportunities to help others and to spread the Word of God. Jesus didn't worry

---

[4] Matthew 14:13

much about the future. He was fully present to what was happening *now*. He did not waste time feeling bad about the past or worrying about the future.

Jesus gave us plenty of advice on how to pray. One day, he said to his followers, "When you pray, go to your inner room, close the door, and pray to your Father in secret."[5] When Jesus said this, he didn't mean we always have to go pray in a real room with a real door being closed. He meant that we should find the quiet place within ourselves. We should shut out the rest of the world when we go to God in private prayer.

Moses: A Great Man of God

Moses was a great leader. One reason he was great was that he helped the Israelite people escape from slavery. But Moses did this in a very unusual way. He didn't do it by having a big army and fighting a big war. He didn't do it by being born a king. And he didn't do it by running for office and becoming president.

He did it with *prayer* and God's help.

You see, God kept telling Moses to go to Pharaoh (the king) and demand the slaves' release. Each time Moses went, God gave him special powers to prove that he was God's messenger. First, Moses turned the river water into blood. But Pharaoh paid no attention. Then God sent swarms of frogs to cover the land. They were *everywhere* — even in people's bowls and ovens! After that, Pharaoh asked Moses to pray to God to remove all the frogs.

---

[5] Matthew 6:6

So Moses prayed, and God got rid of the frogs.

This kind of stuff kept happening. God sent gnats, flies, hail, locusts, darkness in the daytime, and diseases that killed animals. And through all of this, Pharaoh kept promising to let the slaves go if Moses would pray and ask God to remove the problems. Moses kept praying, but Pharaoh kept breaking his promises.

Finally, after lots of praying, hard times, and broken promises, something worked. God sent the clincher: God caused the firstborn child in all the Egyptian families to die but spared the firstborn child in the Israelite families. Only after all of these deaths did Pharaoh finally agree to let Moses and the Israelites go free.[6]

One of the important things this story tells us is that God never abandons those who love. The story also shows that it's good to keep on trying. Don't let failure stop you from going after your goals. Don't let failure keep you from praying, either. If your goal is the right thing to do, God *will* help you reach it, even if it takes awhile.

---

[6] See Exodus, chapters 7 to 12.

Finally, the story shows the importance of keeping in touch with God. Moses himself did not cause the frogs, flies, and everything else to come; but he knew what to do and what to expect because he had been listening to and talking with God. In other words, Moses was *praying*.

Samuel: The Boy Who Heard God Call

Another famous person in the Bible who prayed was Samuel. He was a kid just like you. (That proves you don't have to be a grownup who's been in school for a zillion years before you can be with God in prayer.)

Samuel was a boy who lived with a bunch of holy men because he was going to be a holy man when he grew up. One night while he was in bed, he heard a voice calling him. He thought it was the voice of Eli, a holy man who was his teacher. So Samuel ran to Eli and said, "Here I am." As it turned out, though, Eli hadn't called Samuel, so the boy went back to bed.

But then Samuel heard the voice again. Thinking it surely must be Eli, Samuel ran to the holy man again and said, "Here I am. You called me." Eli again insisted that he hadn't called the boy — and again Samuel went back to bed.

By this time, Samuel might have been getting scared. Maybe he felt silly, too, because he was hearing things that no one else heard. But Eli, being a holy man, realized that Samuel wasn't just scared or hearing things but that God was trying to speak to him. After Samuel came running a third time, Eli said, "Go to sleep, and if you are called, reply, 'Speak LORD, for your servant is listening.' " So Samuel scrambled back to bed and sure enough the voice called to him again. But this time, Samuel answered the way Eli had instructed.

Once the boy did this, God did indeed give him a message about the future.[7]

Mary: The Girl Who Listened to God

Think about a teenage girl you know and admire. She could be your sister, a baby-sitter, your brother's girlfriend... anybody. Got somebody in mind? Okay. Now think about Mary, the mother of Jesus. Did you know that Mary was probably only a teenager when she became Jesus' mother? (People got married and had babies at a younger age back then.)

Thinking about Mary this way can help you understand that she is like someone you know. She's not a cold plaster statue but a real person who lived the way God wanted her to live.

Mary is a good person to remember when you think about listening to God in prayer; she was very good at it. When an angel told Mary that she would be Jesus' mother, Mary said, "May it be done to me according to your word."[8] She *could* have said, "Oh no. Not me. I'm not worthy." She *could* have said, "Oh no. I've never been a mother before. You'd better give the job to a mother with more experience." She *could* have said, "No. I'm not even married yet. People will say bad things about me. You'd better give the job to someone else."

But Mary didn't say any of these things. Even though it sounded really important and quite scary, Mary agreed to be Jesus' mom.

---

[7] See 1 Samuel 3:1-18.
[8] Luke 1:38

Mary always said "yes" to God's will, but that doesn't mean she was weak or that she had no mind of her own. When Jesus performed his first miracle, Mary was there. They were at a wedding, and the wine ran out early. Not good. Mary told Jesus, "They have no wine" and tried to get Jesus to help. Then Mary told the servers at the wedding to do whatever Jesus said. Jesus told the servers to bring him some big jugs of water. Then he turned the water into wine.[9]

This story shows us Jesus' power. It also shows Mary's ability to sense a need and *do* something about it. Doing what is right and good sometimes means stepping forward and speaking up. Mary had the courage to do this.

So remember, if you have a need, try praying with Mary. Just as Mary sensed that Jesus could help when the wine ran out during the party at Cana, Mary can sense your need and tell it to Jesus.

---

[9] See John 2:1-11.

Something to Do
Praying with Your Eyes and Ears

Here are ways you can use your eyes and ears to help you pray.

Eyes Prayer #1: For one whole day, try to look people in the eye when they talk to you. Don't stare, but be careful not to look away or look down when you're talking with someone. When you look someone in the eye, they're likely to listen to you more carefully. Also, when you look someone in the eye, you see more of the real person. The Holy Spirit lives within each human being. It is easiest to see the Holy Spirit when you listen to others and watch their eyes as you talk with them.

Eyes Prayer #2: Even if you're just sitting at the dinner table, on a park bench, or in the backseat of a car, *look* at someone nearby and think about him or her. What do you think it would be like to *be* that person? What is that person doing? How do you think that person is feeling? Could that person use a prayer from you?

Ears Prayer #1: For one whole day, focus on *listening* rather than talking. You needn't be completely silent, but try to be quieter than you usually are, especially if you talk a *lot*. Then, listen to people around you. Listen to the sounds around you. What are folks talking about? How do they feel? Notice how some voices are soft and others are harsh. What other sounds do you hear? Are they sounds from nature, like birds chirping, or mechanical sounds, like a lawn mower running?

Ears Prayer #2: Find a quiet place and imagine that you're hearing some peaceful music being played. Then, make up some music in your head without humming it aloud. Next, think about Jesus walking down a dusty road with his apostles. What does that sound like? How many different sounds are in the scene? What are Jesus and the apostles talking about? What would you like to hear them talk about? What would you like to ask them or tell them? What do you think they'd say in response?

Prayer for Kids Who Wonder If They'll Grow Up to Be Famous

Will I grow up to be famous, Jesus? If I do, that will be pretty neat. When you're famous, lots of people like you and listen to you. Famous people usually make lots of money, too. I may or may not grow up to be famous — I don't know. If I do get to be famous, I still want to remember you. Help me remember that any talents I have are gifts from God. If I don't become famous, that's okay, too. What's most important is that I live to love and help others and to let others love and help me. Like Mary, I will try to listen to your will for my life.

AMEN

❹
Why Do So Many People Want to Do This?
Why People Pray

People all around the world pray. Some pray on their knees; some pray in a sitting position; some pray with their legs all twisted like a tied shoelace. Some bow down very low, laying their chests and arms out before them on the ground. Christians don't have a corner on prayer. People of all different religions pray.

The fact that all kinds of people around the world pray points to something wonderful. It shows that God is everywhere calling people to come closer. Not everyone calls God "God" because people speak different languages, but that's okay. You may call your mother "Mom" while someone else calls her "Mrs. Whatever," and still someone else calls her by her first name. But she's still the same person no matter what you call her.

It's like that with God. The name we give to God is not as important as who God is. If you put together all the love that ever was, is, and will be in the universe, you'll have God. If that's mysterious or hard to understand, don't worry. Most grownups don't completely understand God, either.

Now it can be pretty hard to pray to all the love in the universe. People seem to have an easier time with praying if they can picture God as a person and call that person "Friend" or "Creator" or something like that. That's why some pictures show God as an old man with long white whiskers who hangs out in the clouds. God isn't *really* like that, but people are often helped in understanding things when they have a picture of some sort.

If picturing God as a grandparent kind of person in the clouds helps you pray, good! Keep doing that. If that vision of God doesn't feel right to you, that's okay, too. Many people pray to Jesus instead of God because Jesus was a real-person version of God who came and lived on earth for a while.

Picture God in whatever way works best for you.

Why Do We Pray?

Think for a few moments about animals and what they understand about life. Just as we understand more about animals than animals understand about us, so God understands more about us than we do about God. That doesn't mean we're bad any more than it means that a pet dog, cat, or fish is bad. We understand our pets and help them in ways that they can't help themselves. In a similar way, God understands us and helps us with things that are beyond our abilities.

God wants to be close to us through prayer. Jesus knew that; that's why he often took time out to be alone with his "Father," as Jesus called God. Indeed, Jesus felt so close to God that when he was dying on the cross, he cried out, "Abba!"[10] In English, *Abba* means "Dad," "Daddy," or "Papa." It was as though Jesus, during his most difficult time, cried out "Dad! This is horrible! Please help me!"

Jesus showed us that God is someone to turn to during all the moments in our lives, whether those times are good, bad, or somewhere in between. When we pray, we know God is calling us closer.

---

[10] Mark 14:36

Prayer helps us when we're feeling down. When we don't understand ourselves, others, or things that happen to us, prayer can help us stay calm. When something really good happens, we know prayer is a way to give thanks to God.

Sometimes our feelings — anger, happiness, sadness, fear, or whatever — are so strong that they baffle us. Sometimes we may even feel that we don't really have any control over life. At times like that, we can trust that what does control our lives is a Higher Being, a Great Spirit, God, who is bigger and greater than any of our feelings and problems.

The rest of this chapter contains stories from kids' lives. The stories will help you understand the different reasons people pray and how God is always an important part of life.

Lily Asks God to Help Others

Lily's father has left home and no one knows where he is. He left over a week ago, after having a big fight with Lily's mom. Now Lily's mom is sad — and she gets angry very easily. Lily prays that God will help her mom and dad.

This kind of prayer is called *intercession*. That's a big word that simply means "praying for others." When you intercede in your prayers, that means you are a "go-between" for someone else and God.

John Tells God That He's Sorry

John was having a rock fight in the street with his friends, even though his dad said it was dangerous and that he shouldn't do it. But it was so much fun…until John threw a rock that broke the window of his parents' new car.

John certainly didn't mean to throw a rock through the window — and he was so sorry that he hadn't listened to his dad. John's dad punished him by making him stay in his room for the rest of the day. Before John went to sleep that night, he prayed and told God how sorry he was.

This kind of prayer is called *contrition*. Contrition comes from the word *contrite*. Being contrite means you are sorry about something you've done, and you want to apologize for it. Here is a good prayer (Prayer of Contrition) for times when you want to tell God you're sorry: *O my God, I am sorry for what I have done because I have offended you. I know I should love you above all things. Help me to make up for what I have done, to do better, and to avoid anything that might lead me to do wrong. Amen.*

Chiao Thanks God for Her Talent

Chiao plays the violin. She's very good at it. After months and months of practice, she plays in a recital one night. When she finishes, the audience not only claps but also gives her a standing ovation — that means that everyone stood up while they clapped! She is so stunned that she starts crying tears of joy. Her music teacher gives her some roses. This has never happened before. Chiao bows for the people and smiles, and in her heart she thanks God for giving her the ability to play so well.

This is an easy prayer to understand. Obviously, Chiao has just said a prayer of *thanksgiving*. Prayers of thanksgiving don't have to happen only during times of extreme joy. They can happen any old time. Even if life seems pretty tough, there is usually *something* you can thank God for. Prayers of thanksgiving are especially good to pray when you feel upset about something that has happened to you. They can help you look on the bright side of life.

Paul Needs God's Help to Make Friends

Paul likes to play video games. He can beat just about anyone. He uses most of his allowance to buy the latest games and uses most of his spare time to play them.

One day the TV set breaks down and Paul can't play anymore. While the TV is being fixed, Paul gets bored and mopes around the house.

"Why don't you call a friend and do something?" his dad says.

"I don't feel like it," Paul sulks. But Paul is really disappointed about something else besides the broken TV. He realizes that he doesn't have any friends because he's been playing video games so often. As he sits on the sofa staring into space, he prays that God will hurry up and get the TV fixed. But then Paul sighs and says a different prayer: *God, I need you to help me make some friends.*

Paul has said a prayer of *petition*. That means that he has asked God for something. Prayers of petition are probably some of the most common prayers we say, since we often need lots of help with life.

Cherie Needs God's Help to Forgive Others

Cherie is angry with her mom and aunt Frieda because she has to wear a dumb-looking dress in her aunt Frieda's wedding. Her mom says Cherie must wear the dress, but Cherie hates it; the dress makes her look like a baby. She wears it at the wedding, and afterward, her cousins and uncles tease her about the dress.

Finally, Cherie can't take it anymore. She tearfully cries to her mother, "You *made* me wear this! I hate it. I look *stupid*! I hate you!" Cherie runs out of the reception hall and locks herself in her parents' car.

After a few minutes, Cherie's mom comes out and knocks on the car window. "Let me in," she says. But Cherie won't unlock the doors. Finally, her mom explains from outside, "I didn't want to hurt your aunt Frieda's feelings, Cherie. This was her big day and she really wanted you to wear that dress. I'm sorry, honey. If I had known it would be this bad,

I would have asked Frieda if you could wear something different."

Cherie just looks down at her feet and sniffles.

"I hope you can forgive us," her mom goes on to say. She touches the window near Cherie's face and then walks away.

Cherie looks up to where her mom's hand had been and then hangs her head again. In her heart she prays, *Jesus, am I supposed to forgive them? I don't feel like it. Help me find a way, though, if I should.*

Forgiving others can be very hard. That's why Cherie said this prayer of *forgiveness*. People will sometimes do things you don't like. Sometimes they do it by accident and sometimes they do it on purpose. Either way, you will feel hurt. It's okay to feel hurt or angry at times like this. But if you find yourself holding a grudge for a long time, that's when it's time to seek God's help for forgiving another person. Staying angry or sad for a long time doesn't harm the person who hurt you, but it *does* harm *you*. That's why Jesus said, "Forgive anyone against whom you have a grievance."[11]

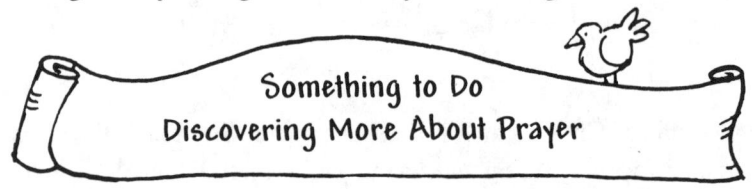

Something to Do
Discovering More About Prayer

Here is a word-find puzzle to help you discover the different things people do and feel as they pray. The words may be printed across (frontward or backward), up and down (frontward or backward), and diagonal (frontward and backward).

---

[11] Mark 11:25

APOLOGIZE	ANGRY	INTERCEDE	HAPPY
BORED	CALM	FRUSTRATED	ASK
THANKFUL	LISTEN	CONCENTRATE	SAD
PUZZLED	RESTLESS	NERVOUS	SMILE
GIVE UP	UPSET	THINK	CRY

S	G	I	V	E	U	P	Z	Z	S	A	D
S	T	N	L	L	C	A	L	M	K	S	E
E	Z	T	H	I	N	K	I	C	F	K	L
L	T	E	C	S	U	O	V	R	E	N	Z
T	O	R	R	T	E	N	U	P	Z	G	Z
S	T	C	Y	E	S	S	I	D	N	I	U
E	S	E	P	N	T	O	E	P	K	Z	P
R	M	D	P	R	H	R	Y	R	G	N	A
O	I	E	A	P	O	L	O	G	I	Z	E
Z	L	T	H	B	Z	Z	U	P	S	E	T
P	E	T	A	R	T	N	E	C	N	O	C
D	L	U	F	K	N	A	H	T	A	I	I

Praying with Popcorn

Just about everybody likes popcorn. Here's a way to use this snack to help you pray. You can do this activity alone, with your family, with your class, or with any small group of people.

Begin with just a bowl of popcorn. As you eat each piece, think of something you would like to thank God for. The things you think of don't have to be big and grand. Ordinary things count, too. Here are some ideas to get you started:

- "Thank you, God, for my good health."
- "Thank you, God, for my family's having enough food to eat today."
- "Thank you, God, for each person who takes care of me." (Eat a piece of popcorn for each person you're thankful for.)

If you're doing this activity with a group of people, each of you can say aloud or silently in your own heart what you're thankful for.

This is a good way of praying if you feel down or left out or not very smart. Popcorn prayer can help you better examine all the good things that God gives you every day.

Prayer for Kids Who Don't Always Feel Like Praying

Jesus, prayer can be hard at times. Sometimes I pray and I feel like it doesn't do much good. Oh, sure, my *brain* says praying always has good results, but my heart doesn't always feel that way. Help me remember that I don't have to always *feel* holy or prayerful to be able to pray. I know you want to hear from me during *all* the times of my life, no matter how I feel. Thank you, Jesus, for loving me just the way I am.

AMEN

❺
What's Your Favorite Flavor?
Different Ways to Pray

Prayer is a little like ice cream. It comes in lots of flavors, but the basic ingredients are the same. Just as all ice cream contains cream and sugar, all prayer involves a person who is spending time with God.

So, exactly how *are* we supposed to pray? Like the kid in the picture below?

> **PRAYER is EASY.** You just get on your knees and say something like "Our Father, who art in Heaven..."

Well, that is the most common way of praying, and it's a fine way to pray. But there are other ways of praying. Getting on your knees and always saying "Our Father, who art in heaven..." can get boring if that's the only kind of praying you do. How would *you* feel if your friend always said the same thing over and over to *you*? You probably wouldn't like it, because you wouldn't learn anything new about your friend's life.

*Hi Julio. You're my best friend!
Hi Julio. You're my best friend!
Hi Julio. You're my best friend...*

If you pray the same way over and over again, maybe you need to find a new kind of prayer that helps make praying more meaningful for you. Maybe you'd feel better spending prayer time with a lady. That's okay. If you want to do that, you can pray with Mary, the mother of Jesus, or with one of the many female saints. You can picture God being like a mother who loves you and wants everything that is good for you. Maybe your back starts to hurt when you kneel. That's okay; you can pray sitting down or standing up. Maybe you can't make it to church to pray. That's okay; you don't have to be in church to pray. God doesn't mind where you pray, even if you're in the bathroom.

There's really only one rule about how to pray: when you pray, do your best to be with God, Jesus, the Holy Spirit, Mary, or any of the saints. That's it. That's the only real rule there is about praying.

Now over the centuries, lots of people have come up with lots of different *ways* of praying and different prayers to say. Remember, though, that you are always free to talk with God about *anything you want* in *any way you want.* That means you don't *have* to use one kind of prayer all the time. You also don't have to use someone else's made-up words to pray.

Yes, there are lots of different ways to pray, and we're going to talk about them next.

The "I-Know-My-Prayers-By-Heart" Method

This kind of prayer you may already know about. When you do this kind of praying, you recite a prayer that you have memorized or can memorize if you want to. Whenever you say the Our Father, Hail Mary, Grace Before Meals, or any other prayer you know by heart, you are using this method.

Here are some of the most popular prayers that people often memorize:

Our Father (The Lord's Prayer)

Our Father, who art in heaven, hallowed be thy name; thy kingdom come; thy will be done on earth as it is in heaven. Give us this day our daily bread; and forgive us our trespasses as we forgive those who trespass against us; and lead us not into temptation, but deliver us from evil. Amen.

Hail Mary

Hail Mary, full of grace. The Lord is with thee. Blessed art thou among women, and blessed is the fruit of thy womb, Jesus. Holy Mary, Mother of God, pray for us sinners, now and at the hour of our death. Amen.

Glory to the Father (Prayer of Praise)

Glory to the Father, and to the Son, and to the Holy Spirit, as it was in the beginning, is now, and will be for ever. Amen.

Grace Before Meals

Bless us, O Lord, and these your gifts, which we are about to receive from your bounty, through Christ, our Lord. Amen.

Thanksgiving After Meals

We give thanks for all your benefits, almighty God, who lives and reigns for ever. May the souls of the faithful departed, through the mercy of God, rest in peace. Amen.

The Creative Method

Do you like to draw, write, sing, or play a musical instrument? Do you like to make things out of clay, wood, or something else? Believe it or not, you can use any of these activities in your prayer life.

Sometimes it can be really hard to talk things over with God. You may be one of those persons who can better tell God what's on your mind by drawing a picture or writing a letter. Maybe you'd like being with God by singing a song, playing music, or creating something else. (Read the short book *The Clown of God*, by Tomie DePaola, for a good story about someone who did this. The book has many beautiful pictures, too. Ask an adult to order this book for you from

Harcourt Brace Jovanovich, Inc., 1250 Sixth Avenue, San Diego, CA 92101. It was published in 1978. The phone number is 800-346-8648.)

Many great artists, musicians, writers, sculptors, and others have used these special ways and their special talents to praise God. You can, too!

The Bible Method

Do you like stories? Do you like to find out about other people's lives? Do you like discovering what life on earth was like a long time ago? Then this method could be for you. The Bible method of praying goes like this: choose a passage from Scripture. Read it slowly and carefully. Then sit back and try to put yourself in the story you just read. Imagine what *you* would have done if you had been one of the main characters in the story.

This type of praying is kind of like sitting back and creating a movie in your head. Add music and sound effects if you want. Think of what the weather was like and even what the smells may have been.

If you'd like to try the Bible method of praying, here is a list of passages to get you started.

- Luke 18:18-23 (The rich official)
- Matthew 15:29-31 (Jesus heals people)
- Daniel 5:1-17, 23-30 (A mysterious hand writes on the wall!)
- Matthew 6:25-34 (Jesus' advice for folks who worry)
- 1 Samuel 3:1-18 (The boy who hears a voice in the night)
- John 2:1-11 (Mary's Son performs his first miracle)

Praying with the Saints and Mary

Do you know what a hall of fame is? You'll usually find halls of fame in sports. Getting into a hall of fame is a big honor, like getting an important medal or trophy or other award. Athletes who make it into a hall of fame get there because they've been very good athletes for many years. Not many people make it into halls of fame. If they do make it, it isn't until they've retired — sometimes not even until they're dead! Hall-of-famers serve as good examples for other athletes who want to play their very best.

The Church has a hall of fame, too. It's called *the communion of saints.* Saints are people who lived such good Christian lives that the Church decided to give them the special honor of sainthood. Saints are to people trying to be good Christians what hall-of-famers are to people trying to be good athletes.

All the saints were people who prayed. The Church also says that the saints are in heaven with God. One special way of praying is praying with a saint. Many churches display statues of saints and a tray of candles nearby. You can light the candles as a symbol of your prayer with that saint.

We don't pray *to* the saints as if they have the power to help us; only God can help us. Instead, we pray *with* the saints; we ask them to *intercede* for us.

> INTERCEDE... ISN'T that when A player from the other team gets the ball from your team?

> No, FuzZ BrAiN! — That's INTERCEPT!

When someone *intercedes* for you, that means he or she sticks up for you. It means that the person comes in to try to help you. This is sort of like how a pinch hitter comes in to bat for another player when the team needs an extra boost. For example, let's say some big creepy boy at school is always teasing you. He keeps trying to pick a fight, and you can't get him to stop. You might tell your mom or dad about it. If your folks talk to your teacher about the problem and try to solve it for you, your folks are interceding for you.

Mary and the saints can intercede for us, too. When we pray with Mary or the saints, we ask them to go to God with us in our prayers. We put our faith in their ability to help us carry our prayer to God.

Many people pray with certain saints about special things. For example, many people pray with Saint Anthony to help them find lost things. They pray with Saint Jude when their problems seem hopeless. They pray with Saint Francis if an animal is sick. People have prayed with Saint Agnes to help young girls, and with Saint Bernadette to help cure illnesses.

There are many other saints who are not as well-known as these (like Saint Thorlac, the patron of Iceland, and Saint Eustachius, the patron of hunters). If you'd like to learn more about saints, there are many books and stories about them. Ask your teacher or one of your parents to help you.

Praying with Affirmations

Affirmation is a big word that simply means saying something that is true. If you say "God loves me and helps me," that's an affirmation. You are saying (*affirming*) that it's true.

Affirmations are unique prayers. Many grownups you know may not have heard of them. These kinds of prayers are short and simple, which makes them great for young people.

Let's say you're sitting at the kitchen table trying to finish your math homework. You're trying and trying, but you just can't figure out how to do the problems. Pretty soon, you get mad and want to throw away the math book. You may think, "Math is stupid! I'm stupid. I just can't do it!"

If you find yourself thinking this way, *stop*! Tell yourself, "Stop!" This kind of thinking doesn't help; it only keeps you stuck! Some people call it "stinking thinking." This is where an affirmation prayer can help. Sit back for a few minutes. Close your eyes. Take a deep breath. Then say to yourself, "Jesus is with me in all I do, helping me find a way to get through." Repeat that statement over and over to yourself for a few minutes as you keep breathing deeply. Try to clear all the anger and frustration from your mind. Simply keep saying to yourself, "Jesus is with me in all I do, helping me find a way to get through." Work to really *believe* this short prayer.

Praying this way won't instantly make you a math whiz, but it can help you calm down, clear your head, and consider new ways of dealing with the problem. This sort of praying also helps you remember that God can do *anything*, even help your poor old brain figure out math.

These little "mini-prayers" are especially good if you find it hard to believe that God cares about you or that there even *is* a God.

The important thing about affirmation prayers is that they always talk about *now*. They are not for praying about the past or the future. A little prayer like "I said something mean to my mom. I'm sorry, please help me make it up to her, Jesus" is a good prayer, but it is not an affirmation. That's because it talks about something you already did (in the past) and something you hope Jesus will do (in the future). But you could change a prayer like that to an affirmation prayer by saying something like "I am thinking of something nice to do for my mom. Thank you, Jesus."

Get the idea? Here are some more affirmations to help you.

- The forgiving love of Jesus helps me find the way to make things better.
- Today, I share God's love with others.
- My life has great value because God loves me.
- The power of God helps me find answers to my problems.
- I am not afraid because the Holy Spirit is with me.

Try to make up some of your own. It's good to have a different one for each day. Say your affirmation over and over many times throughout the day. Praying this way will help you really believe what you're saying and help you feel closer to God.

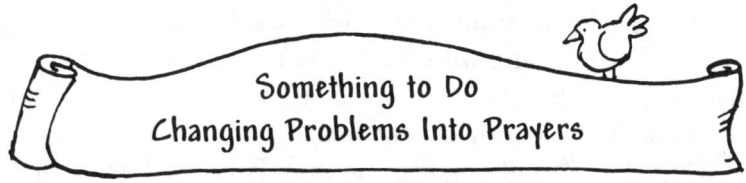

Something to Do
Changing Problems Into Prayers

Below is a list of "stinking thinking" thoughts that many kids can have during an average day. You can change them into affirmations! The first two are done for you. See if you can make up affirmations for the other three.

"Yuk. Another boring day at school."

"God fills my day with many good things."

"None of the kids at school like me."

"Today, I am finding new ways to bring God's love to others."

"I can't do anything right."

_____

_____

"I've never tasted this before. It looks disgusting."

_____

_____

"I have to read something in front of class today. I'm scared! I just can't do it!"

_____

_____

Praying with Objects

When you walk around the block where you live or where you go to school, you usually see the same old buildings, street signs, trees, and so on. But if you walk around the block once a day for a whole month and pay close attention to the surroundings, you would probably notice some things changing. For example, maybe one day you'd notice a man cutting down a dead tree; on another day you might hear someone practicing on the saxophone; on still another day you might notice that the air smells good because someone is barbecuing chicken. You'd see that even though the neighborhood is the same old place, some things about it are always changing, growing, or dying away. That's normal.

Praying with objects can be a little like taking a walk

around the same old block and looking for new things. The following activity will help you understand that.

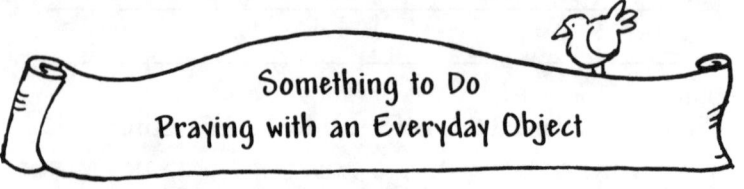

Something to Do
Praying with an Everyday Object

Get one of the following things:

- packing material that has those little bubbles you can pop
- something made of suede
- a coin
- something furry (that's not alive)
- something that smells good
- a piece of tree bark
- a seashell
- a wad of real cotton (not artificial cotton)
- a piece of lace

Now, find yourself a quiet place and just sit with the item in your hand. Close your eyes and invite God to be with you. As you do that, touch the item in your hand…but keep your eyes closed. Feel the object in every way possible. Is it warm or cool? rough or soft? natural or made by people?

Use the object to make up a prayer of thanksgiving. For example, if you are holding a seashell, thank God for the pretty shell. Also thank God for the sea and all the creatures of the sea. Think about the sea and everything about it that is good. Think and pray about what the sea needs; for example, in some places the sea is too dirty and needs to get cleaned up. Ask God how you can help clean up the sea or keep it clean.

If you're holding something made by humans, think of the person or persons who might have made it. Picture them surrounded by a blanket of God's love. Ask God to help them with their struggles in life. Thank God for the work they did to make the object in your hand.

Think of how the object is useful. Could it decorate your room? Could it help a sick person? Could it help get something done? Has it ever protected something or someone?

Praying with objects in this way can help you see the ordinary things in life with new eyes. You'll notice, understand, and think about the things God has made for us in a whole new way. That's part of what prayer is all about! You can use this kind of praying with many other objects, too.

If you're using this book in religion class, the class could break up into groups, depending on which object they're praying with. (For example, all the kids with coins in one group, kids with steel-wool pads in another group, and so forth.)

If you're using this book at home and you want your family to join you, it might be best to have everyone use the same object at one time.

A Classic Prayer Object: The Rosary

A *rosary* is a string of beads that looks a bit like a necklace. It is especially good for praying with Mary, since praying the rosary means saying the Hail Mary *lots* of times. Many kids' parents and grandparents pray with rosaries, but the rosary is for *anyone*, young or old.

Praying the rosary is another one of those "classic" ways of praying. It's sort of like taking a walk around the block with Jesus and Mary.

Praying the rosary is easy to learn. Here's how to do it.

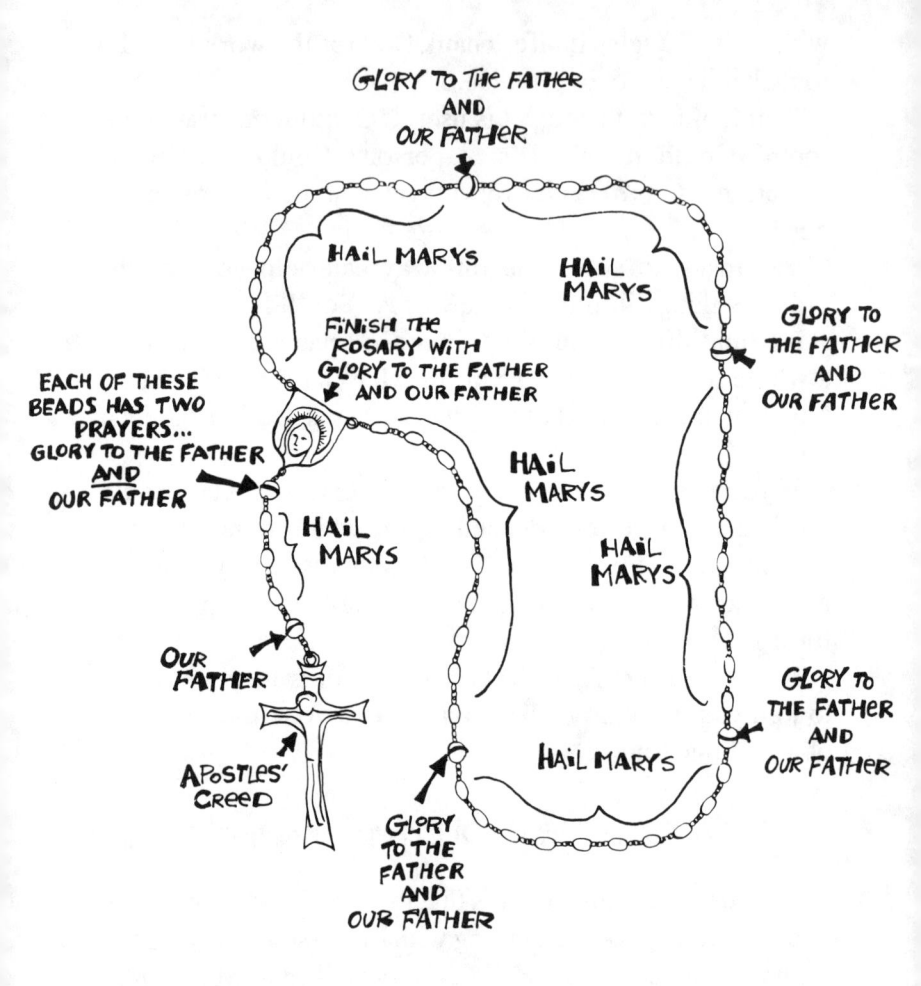

With the cross of the rosary, make the Sign of the Cross on yourself. Next, while still holding the cross in your hand, say the Apostles' Creed. This is a very old prayer that lists all the specific things we believe as Catholics.

Apostles' Creed

I believe in God, the Father almighty, creator of heaven and earth. I believe in Jesus Christ, his only Son, our Lord. He was conceived by the power of the Holy Spirit and born of the Virgin Mary. He suffered under Pontius Pilate, was crucified, died, and was buried. He descended to the dead. On the third day he rose again. He ascended into heaven, and is seated at the right hand of the Father. He will come again to judge the living and the dead. I believe in the Holy Spirit, the holy catholic Church, the communion of saints, the forgiveness of sins, the resurrection of the body, and the life everlasting. Amen.

From there, follow the diagram. While you pray the rosary, think about the happy and sad events that happened to Mary and Jesus. Once you know the basics of praying the rosary, you may be interested in learning that there is even more to it. Ask a grownup who knows about the rosary to help you learn more.

Your Own Way of Praying Is Best

In this chapter you've learned about a lot of different ways to pray. Some you will find useful; others you won't. Remember, though, these aren't necessarily the only ways to pray. There are as many ways to pray as there are people on earth! After all, *somebody* before *you* had to think up all the ways of praying that this chapter talks about. For you, your own way of praying is best. Use your noodle and see what you can come up with.

Prayer for Kids Who Are Ready to Pray

Jesus, there sure are a lot of ways to pray! Now I know I can pray when I'm out playing or walking or waiting to see the doctor or drawing a picture — or doing just about anything. I can even pray when I'm dribbling a basketball or washing my hair. I'm glad I don't *always* have to be on my knees or in church to pray. I'm glad I don't always have to say memorized prayers. Thank you for all the interesting ways to pray and for the people who have created all these ways to pray.

AMEN

6

Is It Really Worth It?

Common Problems With Prayer

Kyle had heard his dad make the promise. His sister had even been there as a witness when the words came out of Dad's mouth: "You can count on me. The next game, I'll be there....*I promise.*"

Dad was a really busy kind of guy, so he could hardly ever be at school plays, recitals, and other things...like Kyle's soccer games. He spent a lot of time on jets, in airports, in hotels, and at meetings...lots and lots of meetings in cities all over the country. Sometimes a phone call would come as early as four-thirty in the morning, and Dad would have to get ready to fly someplace for his job.

"Why can't Dad ever come to my games?" Kyle asked his mom. "This year I'm having a great season. I'm playing real good. Doesn't he want to see me? Doesn't he like me?"

"Honey, of course Dad likes you, and of course he wants to be at your games," said Mom. "But you know about his job. He works hard so he can give us this nice house and nice things, and so we can afford to send you kids to good schools."

"Yes, but this time he *promised.* Dad *promised!* Then this morning he goes flying off again. How can he do that? He lied! *Dad lied to me!* When I lie, I get punished, but Dad gets to lie just because he feels like it!" Kyle was hollering. "Honey, you don't understand...."

"Yes, I do understand! I understand Dad doesn't *care* at all!"

Kyle stomped off to his room and slammed the door. He wanted to take the soccer ball on the bedroom floor and throw it at the window — Kyle was that mad. But instead, he bounced down onto the edge of his bed. He looked all around his room at the nice things Dad had bought for him: baseball caps from all over the country, puppets from around the world, the new bunk beds he'd always wanted, video games, even a computer!

Then Kyle looked at the cross hanging on the wall. He tried praying but found that all he had to say to God was "How can you let this happen? Some God *you* are! You must not be very powerful or else you wouldn't let things like this happen! I don't think you listen to me at all." Kyle figured it wasn't nice to talk to God that way, so he gave up trying to pray. He just buried his head into his pillow as tears rolled down his cheeks.

Prayer Problem #1
Yeah, But What If I'm Angry with God?

When you're praying, you're supposed to be nice and kind and quiet and peaceful and love God and everyone around you and not think anything mean...right?

Well...*maybe.* If you think you're never supposed to be mad when you're praying, here's some news:

**God Would Rather Hear
From You When You're Mad
Than Not Hear From You At All.**

Does that surprise you? It may be hard to believe, but God would rather hear you say "God, you're a jerk. How could you let this happen! It's not fair!" than not hear from you at all.

There are some good folks in the Bible who got mad at God. Moses got mad when he had to lead the Israelites through the desert for forty years — imagine that, *forty years.* The people were hungry and crabby, and Moses got pretty fed up with them.

"Why do you treat your servant so badly?"[12] Moses asked God. He was upset and let God know it.

Yes, Moses told it to God straight. Moses showed us that it's always better to tell it like it is to God rather than covering up anger or other feelings with phony niceness. You see, God isn't like human beings. God doesn't get angry — and God's feelings don't get hurt when people pray with anger. So if you're mad at God, go ahead, be mad. God can take it. God can also use your anger to help you deal with whatever it is that made you angry in the first place.

Another Bible person who got angry with God was Sarai. Sarai also got mad at her husband, Abram, and her maidservant. Sarai was angry because God promised Abram and her that they would have lots of children. But time dragged on and on and on, and still no children. So Sarai got angry and turned away from God.[13]

---

[12] Numbers 11:11
[13] See Genesis 15–16:6.

The important thing to remember about anger and prayer is that if you *feel* nice and kind, that's great! Go ahead and pray. But if you're like most folks, there are times when you're so upset that prayer is about as far from your mind as an elephant is from the South Pole. Anger is normal, and God wants to hear about it when you're angry, even if you're angry with God.

The most important thing about being angry with God (or anyone else) is that you eventually get over it. Think about the last time you got mad at your brother or sister or mom or dad. When you get mad at those people, your anger doesn't go on forever, does it? For most of us, anger eventually settles down and passes. That's a good way for it to be with God, too. So go ahead and get mad at God if you feel like it. But don't hold onto the anger forever.

Prayer Problem #2
Yeah, But What If God Doesn't Always Answer My Prayer?

Use your imagination for a few moments here. Think back to a time when you had something really important to tell someone, but they weren't listening to you. Maybe you were trying to tell Mom about a great program on TV, but she was trying to drive through rush-hour traffic and was distracted. Maybe you were trying to tell your teacher about how your dog had puppies, but he was trying to make the class settle down and was busy. Maybe you were trying to tell your sister about the part you got in the school play, but she was getting ready to go out with her friends and was more interested in her makeup.

Write how you felt about that person not listening to you.

_____

_____

_____

Now, think about a time when you prayed very hard for something — a time when you felt like telling God, "God, *please* do this for me. If you'll do this *one* thing for me, I promise to make it up to you. I *promise.*" If you'd like, you can write what it was you prayed for.

_____

_____

_____

Did God give you exactly what you prayed for? If so, that's great. If you're like most folks, though, there have probably been times when you thought God didn't come through for you. You may have thought, "God isn't listening to me" or "I wonder if there *is* a God."

If you've thought these things, you're not alone, and you're not bad for thinking that God's not listening. *Lots* of people have thought this. Even some people in the Bible thought God wasn't listening. Job (pronounced JOBE) was one of those guys. Job had some really *big* problems. Thugs came in and slaughtered his oxen, camels, and donkeys, as well as many of his servants. Fire killed all his sheep. A tornado killed all ten of his children at the same time! If that wasn't enough, Job got a really yucky disease that left his whole body covered with sores and scabs. Yes, Job was in bad shape and had every right to ask God, "Aren't you listening to me? Help!" In fact, he did complain to God when he said, "Oh, that I had one to hear my case!...This is my final plea; let the Almighty answer me!"[14]

The remarkable thing about Job, though, is that no matter how bad life got, he still believed in God. Long after most of us would have given up, Job kept trusting that God had a plan for his life. In the end, Job got everything back and more. His disease went away, and his brothers and sisters had a big party with him. They gave him money and a gold ring. Later, Job had more children and got many sheep, camels, oxen, and donkeys again. Job then lived to be old enough to see his great-grandchildren.

So the next time you think God has a hearing problem, think about Job. He, too, wondered if God was listening. His story shows us that God is always listening, but sometimes God has different things in mind than what we ask for.

Jesus once said, "Ask and it will be given to you; seek and you will find; knock and the door will be opened to you."[15] When he said this, he was talking about praying for God's

---

[14] Job 31:35, 37

[15] Matthew 7:7

help. It might seem like Jesus was telling a "tall tale," particularly if you continue to pray about something and feel like you're getting no answer. If that happens, remember that God's plan isn't always the same as your plan. This sort of thing happens to people every day. For example, it may seem like Mom's not listening to you when she's driving, but she has something better in mind: your safety! She wants to get you there safely, and so does God.

Prayer Problem #3
Yeah, But What If I Don't Have Time to Pray?

Time is a funny thing. When you need lots of time, there often isn't enough. When you want time to go fast (like when you're waiting for the school bus that's late and it's cold outside), time crawls like a tired turtle.

But here's a secret about time that a lot of people don't know. Are you ready to hear it? Okay, here goes…

YOU CONTROL YOUR TIME!

Does that secret surprise you? Maybe you think that your parents and teachers and coach and mean big brother control your time, not you. But think about this as an example: when you go to school every day, you are *choosing* to go to school. You *could* choose to skip school, but you choose not to.

(Probably because you'd be dead meat if you did!) You may think it's your parents who make you spend time cleaning your room, or it's your teacher who forces you to do homework. But when it comes right down to it, *you* are the one who chooses to do these things. You can always choose *not* to do them, although there is usually BIG TROUBLE coming your way for doing that.

Many people don't pray because they say they *don't have time*. That's a shame, because praying doesn't *have* to take a lot of time. In fact, it's quite possible to pray while you're doing something else. Saint Therese of Lisieux did this. She was a girl who did a lot of praying while doing regular things like scrubbing floors.

Look at the list below and put a checkmark in front of those activities or chores that you might do during an average week.

- ☐ doing dishes
- ☐ tying your shoelaces
- ☐ waiting for or riding the school bus
- ☐ mowing the lawn
- ☐ eating
- ☐ taking a shower or bath
- ☐ riding a bicycle
- ☐ something else (write that on the line below)

_____

Believe it or not, each of these things provides a good time for praying. Just ask God to be in your heart while you're doing these things — or anything else.

Something to Do
Creating Time for Yourself

Here are some lists for you to complete. Filling in the blanks will help you know who and what's most important to you.

The three most important people in my life are (it's okay to include yourself, if you like)
1. _____
2. _____
3. _____

The three most important things my parent(s) and teacher(s) want me to do are
1. _____
2. _____
3. _____

The three most important things that I like to do are
1. _____
2. _____
3. _____

The three most important things God wants me to do or be are (the first one is filled in for you)
1. _pray_____
2. _____
3. _____

Now, if you have trouble finding time to pray, ask yourself this question: "Are there things I regularly spend time doing that aren't on any of the above lists?" If so, write them here:

1. _____

2. _____

3. _____

If you want to find time to pray, consider doing less of whatever you wrote on the blank above. Begin by just trying to find five quiet minutes every day to spend some time with God. This could mean getting out of bed a few minutes earlier in the morning, watching five minutes less of TV, or something else. Use your imagination!

Now, guess what you just did. You just set some *priorities*. Setting priorities means figuring out what's most important by deciding how to spend your time. If you can learn to do this now, it will help you a *lot* when you grow up.

Sticking with priorities isn't always easy, though. Your friend may say, "Come over to my house and we can watch *Return of the Meat-Hook Murderer* on cable TV!" But you can say, "No, thanks, I want to _____ instead." It won't be easy to say this, but it's the right thing to do. God doesn't want you to go along with things you don't like just because your friends want you to.

Prayer Problem #4
Yeah, But What If People Think I'm Weird?

If you have this problem, go back and review pages [23-28]. These pages talk about just this topic.

Prayer Problem #5
Yeah, But What If I Can't Concentrate When I Pray?

No one can force you to pray. Even if someone marches you into church and orders you to kneel and be quiet and pray, that doesn't mean you will pray. Instead, you may stare at the pattern on the back of another kid's jacket and wonder where he got that neat jacket. You might look at the baptismal font and wonder if there's water in it and how long it's been there. Your mind may wander to how you're kneeling right where Alvin Schneiderhoeffer got sick in church once, so you're wishing you could kneel someplace else.

If your mind wanders like this, you have a problem that many folks (grownups included) have when they pray. If you have this problem, remember these important points.

People pray best when they pray with their hearts, not just their minds. If you find your mind wandering, try to concentrate on how your heart feels. That means telling God how you feel (angry, happy, bored, and so on) and why.

God always appreciates it when you pray or try to pray. If you fear that you're not praying perfectly, don't worry about it. The fact that you're trying is what's important to God.

With prayer, sometimes you have good days and sometimes you have blah days. Praying can be like practicing the piano or practicing so you can play a better ball game. When you practice at any of these things, some days will be good and other days will not be so hot. Some days you'll concentrate well; other days you won't. That's normal for everyone who prays.

Don't give up on prayer. If you get discouraged with prayer, try not to give up. If prayer gets really tough, try talking about the problem with someone who knows a lot about prayer. This may be your mom, dad, grandparents, godparents, or a priest, Sister, Brother, or deacon; any of these may be able to help you.

Get Ready for Results!

When people who haven't been praying much start praying regularly, something wonderful usually happens. Angry people find themselves cooling down. Sad people find themselves feeling better. Frightened people feel less afraid.

Get ready for something like this to happen to you, too, if you begin praying regularly. That's because *prayer changes things!* Oh, you can't use prayer like a magic wand to change a D to an A on a report card. And you can't use prayer to zap someone into being your best friend if he or she doesn't really like you. But prayer *is* mysteriously wonderful. More than anything, prayer will change *you*. It will change you for the better. When you talk with God, Jesus, Mary, the Holy Spirit, or any of the saints in prayer, they'll help you see the world God's way. Prayer helps you act, think, and feel like a good person who loves others as Jesus did. Prayer helps you put on "God-colored glasses."

Something to Do
Learning More About Prayer

This puzzle will help you learn more about prayer.

ACROSS
3. Old Testament man who kept praying and having faith, even though many bad things happened to him and his family.
5. Prayer is _____ with God.
7. Where can prayer happen?
8. Famous boy who prayed in the Old Testament.
11. When you say a prayer of petition, you are _____ for something.
12. Jesus took the _____ to pray.

DOWN
1. When you say a prayer of contrition, you are _____.
2. When you pray with Mary or the saints, they _____ for you.
4. Sometimes what you want and what God wants are not the _____.
6. When you pray, you talk to God and _____ to God.
7. When is God with you?
9. Old Testament man who got angry with God.
10. Prayer is not just words. It's also an _____.

Prayer for Kids Who Find Praying Hard to Do

Sometimes, Jesus, it's hard to pray. Was it ever like that for you? Did you ever get so angry that you felt like punching out someone's lights instead of praying? Did you ever get so pooped at the end of the day that you wanted to say, "Later, God. I'm too tired." When you were a little boy, Jesus, did your mind ever wander to thinking "What's for dinner?" while you were trying to pray? Did your friends ever say you were weird because you sometimes wanted to pray instead of play?

I don't know if you had those problems, but I sometimes do. At times, my poor brain wants to keep thinking about other things. Sometimes I feel so mixed up that I don't know where to begin. Sometimes the day gets so busy that finding a few minutes to talk with you is like trying to find pennies in the ocean.

But even though I may find it hard to be with you, I know that *you* are always with me, Jesus. Thank you for that. I'm sorry about the times I've stayed away from talking with you when I was angry, busy, or afraid. Please help me and other kids come closer to you in prayer.

AMEN

AMEN

Life is full of many little things that no one pays much attention to — things like aglets, jambs, and flews.

Aglets, jambs, and flews are things we see just about every day, but most people call them "thingamajigs, doohickeys, and whatchamacallits." But without aglets, you couldn't tie your shoes. Without jambs, you couldn't walk through a doorway. And without flews (not fleas), hound dogs would look really WEIRD! Look up these words in a dictionary and use them occasionally; you'll really impress your parents and friends!

The word *amen* is also one of those everyday little things that no one pays much attention to. But people would really miss it if it weren't around! *Amen* sounds like a holy way of saying *The End.* But it means more than that.

People have been saying "amen" since before Jesus lived on earth. It was the Hebrew way of saying "certainly." Over time, it also came to mean "so be it," "we agree," and "it is so."

Now you know.
Don't you feel smart?

AMEN!